YORK

THE GREAT CITY

Chris Gee

HALSGROVE

First published in Great Britain in 2016

British Library Cataloguing-in-Publication Data
A CIP record for this title is available from the British Library

ISBN 978 0 85704 296 5

HALSGROVE
Halsgrove House,
Ryelands Business Park,
Bagley Road, Wellington, Somerset TA21 9PZ
Tel: 01823 653777 Fax: 01823 216796
email: sales@halsgrove.com

Part of the Halsgrove group of companies.
Information on all Halsgrove titles is available at: www.halsgrove.com

Printed in China by Everbest Printing Investment Ltd

INTRODUCTION

Shhh ... don't tell my folks back home in Lancashire, but I love this city.

I first got to know York in the early 1980s when I was still at junior school, I guess in much the same way as many people first got to know York, on day trips to see the sights and the museums.

The local authority where I then lived, chartered a train to take schoolchildren from schools across Salford to York for the day. I can still recall details from that day trip: a tour of the Castle Museum and National Railway Museum; a sunny picnic in the gardens between Leeman Road and the River Ouse and climbing up to Clifford's Tower. We must have been studying medieval or Tudor history on the curriculum at the time and our teachers probably thought York would be a great place to absorb some of what we were studying. Not the first time in history that a gang of marauding Lancastrians has descended on York!

And what a great idea that was. I can't think of a better place in the British Isles that so encapsulates British history, particularly the sort young children are interested in. Romans, Vikings, the medieval period, the Tudors and the War of the Roses, the Civil War and all those great icons (heroes and villains?) of childhood history lessons: Henry VII, Richard III, Guy Fawkes, Dick Turpin. And they make chocolate here too!

King George VI once said that the history of York is the history of England. A great observation and we are fortunate indeed that so much of historic York has been preserved. A walk through the city can take you back in time almost 2000 years (and beyond if you know where to look).

About four years ago I took up a new post in York, moved lock, stock and barrel from the other side of the Pennines, set up home with my future wife and fell in love with the place we now call home.

York is such a contrast to my childhood home, a city yes, but with a much more intimate feel than the twin conurbations of Salford and Manchester where I grew up. York is much smaller too, such that it's the kind of place best explored on foot (or pushbike) and it's easy to stride from one side of the city to the other in a good twenty minutes, the heart of the city being less than a mile across.

I've spent much of the last four years on foot, exploring every quarter of this fine city. What makes York so special is that every visit reveals something new. Having lived here for four years now, I'm still finding hidden gems, little surprises as I turn a corner or duck down an alleyway I've never explored before. Sometimes the sun can light up a view in a different way, shining a light on something that I haven't spotted before. In fact, knowing where to look is key and looking up is important too, raising your eyes above street level can reveal detail easily missed if you rush across the city with your head down.

There are the obvious attractions: York Minster, Clifford's Tower and the Shambles, but there are lots of hidden backstreets that can reveal over-hanging medieval buildings and numerous snickelways, a wonderful term coined by the author Mark W. Jones, who devised a circuit around York using these snickets, ginnels and alleyways. There is wonder in the detail too, from old shop signs and street furniture that have somehow survived the ages, to the remains of a Norman house, the foundations of a Saxon church and old Roman walls.

I never tire of a tour of the city walls. At just under 3 miles, it's a good lunchtime circuit and offers a wonderful perspective on the city. They are the best preserved city walls in England and while much of what we see today dates to restoration in the eighteenth and nineteenth centuries, the basic foundations and line of the walls dates to the mid thirteenth century and in some cases Roman times.

There are few tall buildings within the city walls which allows the Minster to dominate the cityscape. The walls also offer a view across the rooftops, a chance to count the amazing number of churches within the city walls, though the number of churches is still eclipsed by the number of pubs.

Better still is the climb up to the top of Clifford's Tower or, even better, the heart busting climb to the top of the tower of York Minster for a view that takes in the red-tiled roofs of the city just below and across the wider city to the North York Moors and Yorkshire Wolds to the north and east. The Minster has been dominating the city landscape for almost 550 years and as you approach York from the west or east on the A64, only the tower of the Minster gives away the presence of the city.

York is a city that changes through the seasons, from the first snowdrops that carpet the many churchyards in late January, to the flowering of crocuses in the Museum Gardens, to the wonderful display of daffodils and tree blossom in March, April and May. Daffodils cover the bailey of Clifford's Tower and the grassed embankments below the city walls, a beautiful show of colour early on a spring morning.

Perhaps the seasonal event that surprised me most was the flooding. I knew that York flooded, I'd seen it often enough on the television, but having moved here I hadn't anticipated how often that happened, the river bursting its banks on at least half a dozen occasions in each of the years I've been here. In fact 2012 and 2015 have seen record levels and while in the main the city copes well with the flooding immediately around the Ouse banks, the December 2015 floods were exceptional and devastating for homes and businesses around both the Rivers Ouse and Foss. There's a morbid fascination in watching the slow-moving Ouse flowing under the Ouse Bridge, the waters covering places I often walk at other times of year.

I realised when putting together this collection of photos that I take most of my photos of York between October and April. This is when the light is at its best and the colours too, from the Autumn hues, to the frosty mornings and the first colours of spring. The city is busy all through the year. While there are more visitors during the summer months, York is an all-weather, all-year attraction and the city offers plenty of events and attractions through the autumn and winter months.

Another highlight for me is York Illuminated, when various parts of the city are illuminated in often dramatic and innovative ways. The city is a real pleasure to explore after dark, softening some of the harsher aspects of modernity that have infused the city, helping the visitor glimpse more of the character of old medieval York.

The city takes on a different character after dark, a great time to explore the wonderful pubs and restaurants or perhaps to take a ghost walk. Is there another city in England that can lay claim to so many haunted buildings? York's ghosts seem to be particularly fond of frequenting the local pubs! I haven't seen one yet.

York must also have one of the highest concentrations of museums outside of London and there is something to fascinate every interest: railways, Vikings, the history of York itself, chocolate, farming, aircraft, Richard III, Henry VII, geology, textiles, Roman history and medieval history. They are all covered.

While there have been planning mistakes in the past, particularly during Victorian times and in the 1960s, we've been fortunate that much of old York has survived. Although lots of what we see today has been renovated, refurbished and reconstructed, particularly through the Georgian and Victorian eras, we are indeed lucky that there are enlightened organisations like the York Civic Trust and York Conservation Trust who refresh the old buildings for a modern purpose, while retaining the character that makes York such a special place.

Since I moved across, I've been devouring the history, scouring bookshops for new insights into this wonderful city as it helps to appreciate York all the more if you better understand the past and all that has happened here.

It is a city that has seen constant change and yet in many ways remains unchanged. The Romans called it Eboracum and references to Ebor remain strong, giving the name to an annual horse race event as well as a long distance footpath. The name has changed over time, from Saxon Eoforwick to the Norse Jorvik. The origins of the name, as well as the origins of the city, can be clearly traced through time.

York can be a busy, bustling place at any time of year. The city is popular with visitors all year round these days, yet there are still plenty of open spaces that offer a relaxing retreat from the hustle and bustle of the streets. Dean's Park and Rowntree Park and even the city wall circuit can offer an oasis of calm if you need to escape the busier, narrow streets.

Today York combines its history with all that a modern visitor expects: restaurants, bars and cafés, designer shops and great music venues. The city balances these roles really well.

I quickly realised when collating the photographs for this book that there is so much more to York. It was a real challenge to decide what to leave in and what to take out. There are so many great buildings and views, that it has proved an almost impossible task to cover comprehensively every detail of the city.

The other thing that struck me was that almost all these photographs were taken in a relatively small area, no more than about 3 square miles. There is so much more beyond the immediate city limits: great countryside, chocolate box villages and wonderful wildlife.

York has to be one of our finest preserved cities in the UK. We should treasure York, it's our heritage and our history. It's a great city.

Chris Gee,
York, 2016

Inset: The Coat of Arms of York was first developed during the reign of Edward III when York was briefly the capital of England at the height of the wars with Scotland. The cross of St George and the Five Lions reflect the honour bestowed on York for its support for the monarchy. The mace and sword represent the city's powers of self-government under the Lord Mayor.

CHAPTER 1

WITHIN THE CITY WALLS, SOUTH OF THE RIVER

Micklegate Bar has long been the traditional point of arrival in the City of York, used by serving monarchs throughout its 800 year history. The bar dates from the early twelfth century. The upper storeys were added in the late fourteenth century.

It was traditionally used to hang the rotting heads and corpses of those traitors who had met an unfortunate end on the gallows. Famous victims include Sir Henry 'Hotspur' Percy in 1403 and Richard Plantagenet, Duke of York, in 1461. The shields on the outer wall date to around 1350 and include two versions of the City of York coat of arms and the royal arms.

Along with Bootham and Monk Bar, Micklegate Bar lost its barbican in 1826 as the Victorian city fathers sought to ease the pedestrian flow through the bars. Today the bar houses the Henry VII Experience, a museum with a particular focus on the War of the Roses.

The city walls between Micklegate Bar and the corner Sadler Tower largely date to the thirteenth and fourteenth century and are the most complete surviving example of medieval city walls still standing in Britain today. Built largely of locally quarried magnesian limestone, they have their origins in the Roman occupation, but have been much altered over the years.

The wall section between Micklegate Bar and Baile Hill offers excellent views across the rooftops to York Minster. There are few high-rise buildings inside the city walls and from this section, the views across the terraces of Bishophill to the Minster are unhindered.

The city walls are locked at dusk and reopened at dawn, though remain closed if conditions are icy. Many sections thankfully remain unfenced and you can spot the tension when passers by take the drop side!

Baile Hill or Old Baile are the remains of the second Norman motte and bailey castle. York was unusual in Britain in having two motte and bailey castles, a measure of how critical the Normans viewed the defence of the city. Old Baile quickly fell into disuse and by 1722 the top was flattened and trees planted on its crown.

Micklegate is regarded by many as the most graceful street in York as it sweeps elegantly up the hill from the Ouse to Micklegate Bar. A climb up Micklegate is a reminder that York is certainly not a flat city. Micklegate retains its cobbled surface and is lined with attractive Georgian houses. This is where York's gentry made their homes in the early eighteenth century, though today Micklegate is a thriving mix of independent shops, cafés and pubs.

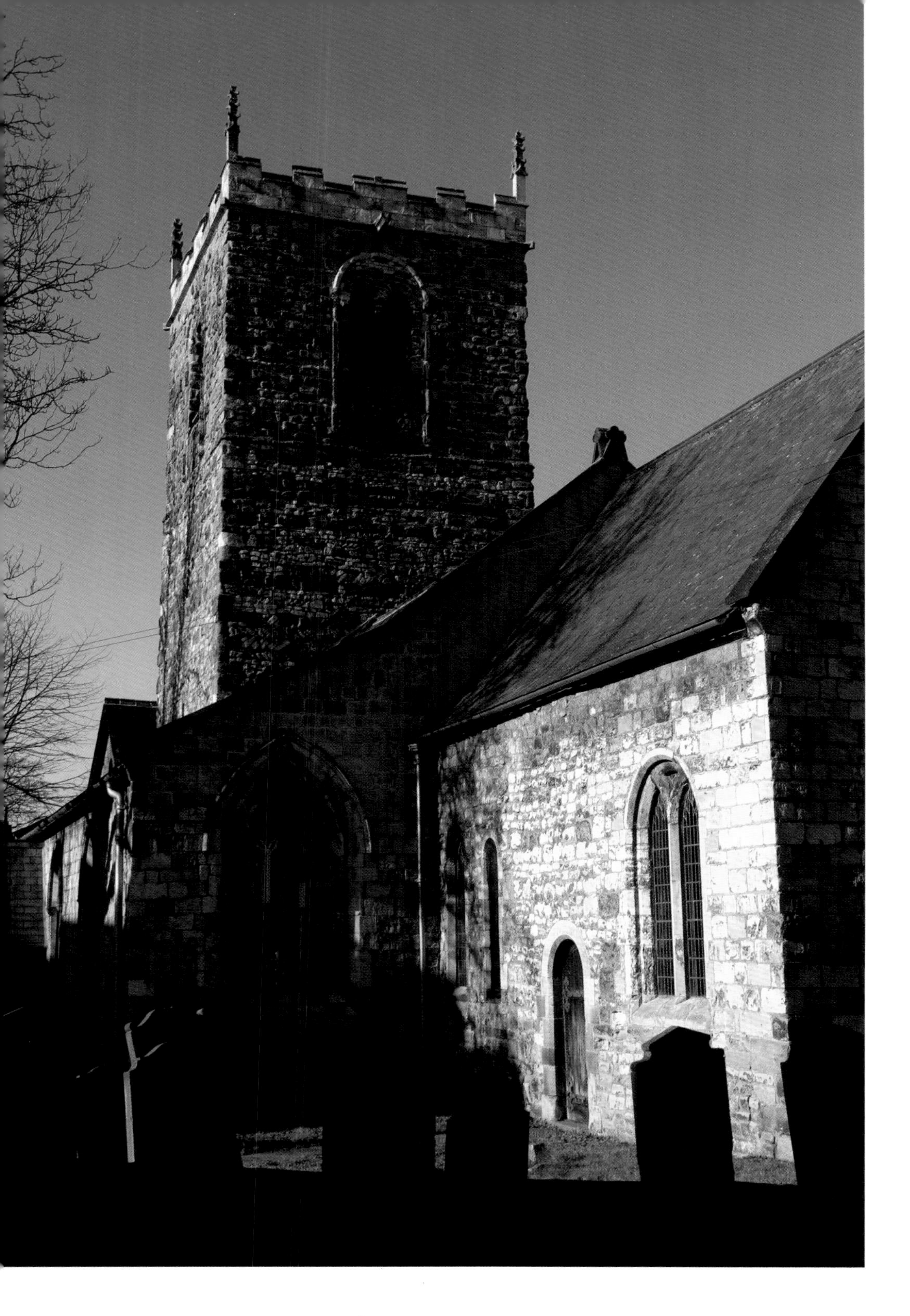

St Mary's church, Bishophill Senior, incorporates the oldest Saxon church tower in York, with much of the lower section dated to the eleventh century and built using Roman stonework. York citizens were clearly early advocates of recycling using building materials from the ruins of the Roman city.

Ann Middleton's Hospital was first built in 1659, but extensively rebuilt between 1827 and 1829. The white painted lady in puritan dress is Ann Middleton. Today the building is a hotel.

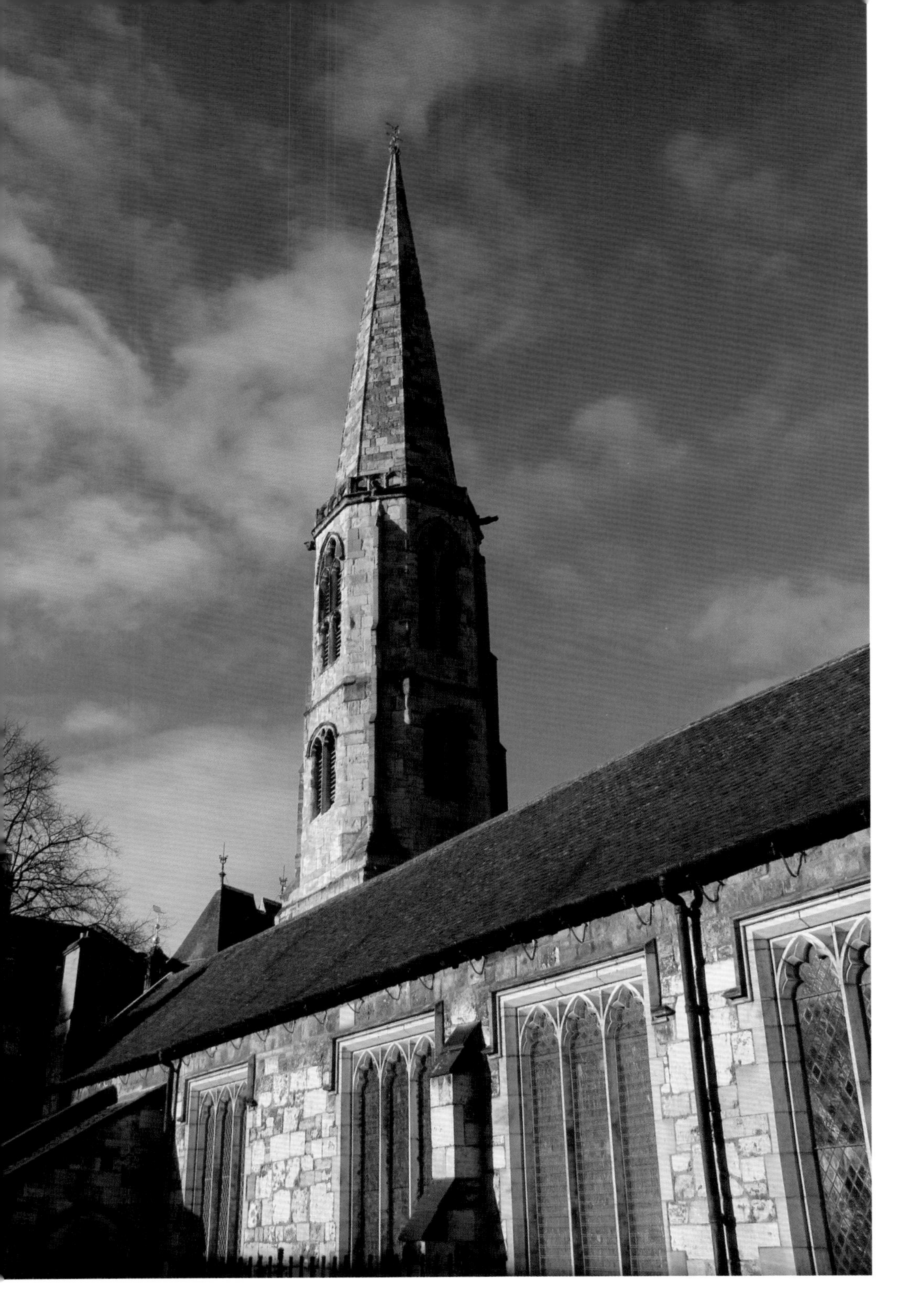

Church Cottages in North Street were built in the fifteenth century, some of the last survivors of medieval timber-framed houses which were once common on North Street, but demolished during the 1950s and 1960s.

Left: All Saints church, North Street, has eleventh-century origins and even incorporates some Roman stonework from a long-vanished building. The church was mostly enlarged in the thirteenth and fifteenth centuries when the tall slender tower was added. This was later topped with the tall spire that dominates the cityscape south of the river. The church has some of the best medieval stained glass in York.

This was York's second railway station, built in Toft Green in 1840 in an Italianate style by G.T. Andrews, the York and North Midland Railway architect. Based within the city walls, its location soon became impractical and the third, current station was built outside the walls in 1877. The old station remained in railway use as offices until after the millennium when it was sympathetically restored and is now used by the City of York Council as their main offices.

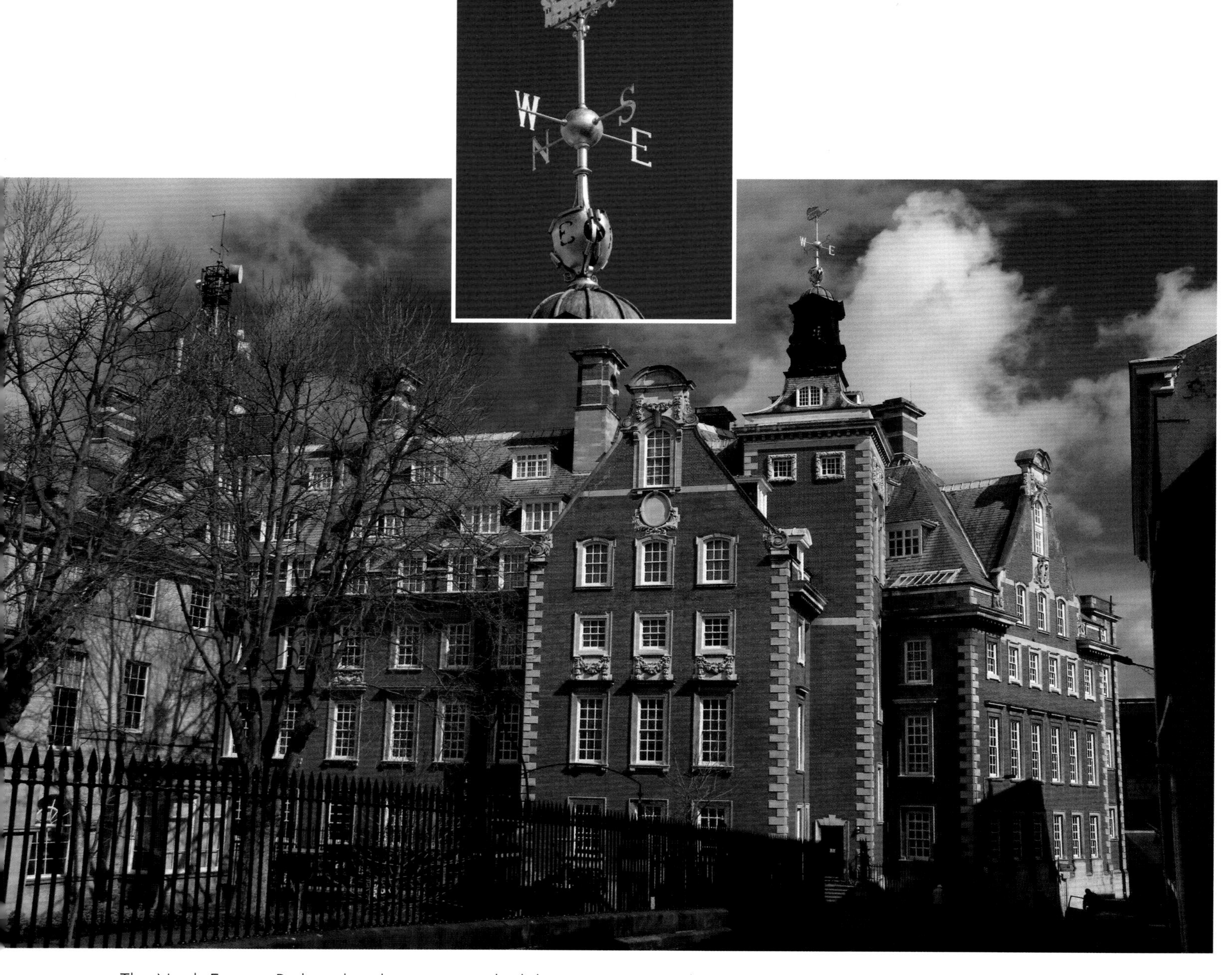

The North Eastern Railway headquarters was built between 1900 and 1906, an opulent building with oak panelled boardrooms. A mark of the confidence and wealth of the North Eastern Railway, the building remained in railway use for over one hundred years as offices until it became a hotel in the new millennium.

The Victorians thought nothing of piercing the city walls for practical purposes, the first occasion in 1839-1840 and then again in 1845 to allow the railway to reach the station at Toft Green. The Victorians breached the walls again in 1874 and 1876 for new roads to reach the new Lendal Bridge.

The section of city wall between Micklegate Bar, particularly between the corner Tower of the Tofts and Leeman Road offers excellent views of York Minster dominating the cityscape.

Little changes in York: this view of the city walls with daffodils was painted for a 1950s' British Railways poster advertising York as a day trip destination by rail. Sixty years later, the view remains unchanged, and daffodils continue to carpet the embankment every spring, a lovely time of year to tour the city walls.

CHAPTER 2
DOWN BY THE RIVER OUSE

Built in the fourteenth century, Barker Tower, also known as North Street Postern Tower, was used to secure the huge iron chain that stretched across to Lendal Tower seen on the north bank. The chain was in place during the Middle Ages and used to enforce river tolls on the Ouse.

Left: One of many warehouses that served the river traffic on the Ouse; like so many in this part of York, this example in Skeldergate now serves another purpose as a recreational gym.

Lendal Bridge was opened in 1863, largely due to increased road traffic after the opening of the railway brought more and more people into the city. A rope-ferry had previously plied the river crossing and when the bridge opened, the ferry operator was gifted a horse and cart as compensation for his loss of business.

An earlier attempt to bridge the river at Lendal in 1860 met with disaster when the bridge collapsed during construction, killing five workers. The bridge and its tollhouses are today listed as Grade II buildings.

Ouse Bridge was opened in 1820 and links Bridge Street with Low Ousegate. It replaced an earlier sixteenth-century bridge which had collapsed into the Ouse, probably due to the weight of all the shops that lined the bridge on both sides.

park inn

Queens Staith was built in 1660 and extended in 1678. As river traffic on the Ouse grew, the staith was extensively rebuilt in the nineteenth century when most of the warehouses that line the quay were built.

Woodsmill Quay warehouse was built between 1860 and 1870.

As has happened across much of Britain and Europe, the riverside warehouses by the Ouse have been converted into apartments and offices as the appeal of living and working in a waterfront property has grown in recent decades. It doesn't come without risk as the cellars of some of these warehouses regularly flood and on occasion access from Skeldergate can be blocked when the Ouse rises particularly high.

Woodsmill Quay on Queens Staith bears the brunt of the rising waters of the River Ouse when it is in flood. Although York itself is on the drier eastern half of the UK, when heavy rain falls on the Yorkshire Dales, North Pennines and North York Moors, the Rivers Swale, Ure, Nidd, Foss and Derwent all combine to overwhelm the river banks in the centre of the city. Two gantry cranes survive on Queens Staith, used to unload cargo from river boats into the adjacent warehouses. As recently as the 1960s, this was a working quayside, but changing transport economics have seen the commercial river traffic diminish and now it is typically leisure craft that tie up at the moorings on the quayside.

The River Ouse has its origins in the River Ure which rises in the North Pennines near Hawes and runs 129 miles through Wensleydale and the Vale of York to join the Humber down river. As the river drains much of upland Northern England, when heavy rain falls on both the Pennine Hills and the North York Moors, much of it finds its way down to York and in the last twenty years river height records continue to be broken.

The Romans established Eboracum on the Ouse because it offered a strategic position on the river with good navigable access to the Humber and the North Sea. The Romans were the first to bridge the Ouse at York, linking Stonegate (Via Praetoria) to Micklegate. The Vikings replaced the Roman structure with a wooden bridge, a little further downstream and closer to where the Ouse Bridge is today. It was not until Victorian times that multiple river crossings were achieved with the opening of Skeldergate Bridge and Lendal Bridge, along with the Scarborough Bridge carrying the railway line.

Skeldergate Bridge was built between 1878 and 1880 at a cost of £56,000. Built largely of cast iron with stone pillars, the bridge has an opening section to allow tall ships to pass through, though this is long disused.

Skeldergate Bridge was declared free of tolls in April 1914 and as is the case with its sister bridge at Lendal, the tollhouse is now a café. The whole structure and tollhouse is a Grade II listed building.

Skeldergate Bridge links Castle Mills with Baile Hill and is the start of the New Walk, a tree-lined avenue created in the 1730s when it became fashionable to take the air, to stroll and to socialise. The walk is still popular today and the new Millennium Footbridge downstream has opened up an opportunity for a circular walk using both riverbanks.

The Greyfriars, or Franciscan Order, first arrived in York in 1230. Nothing survives of the old Franciscan Friary apart from the crenellated walls which date to about 1290 and now provide some limited level of protection against the rising floodwaters of the Ouse to the terraced housing in Friargate.

South Esplanade is home to a terrace of Grade II-listed townhouses.

Davy Tower dates to the fourteenth century, though the summer house on top is an eighteenth-century addition. As with Barker Tower and Lendal Tower, the tower was used to anchor the iron chain that was hung across the Ouse to enforce river tolls on shipping traffic during the Middle Ages.

Cumberland House was built around 1710 for William Cornwall, a prominent York businessman with interests in both tanning and brewing. Cornwall was twice elected Lord Mayor in 1712 and 1725.

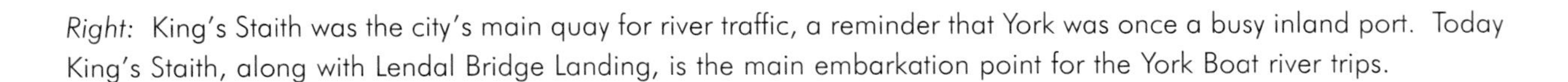
Right: King's Staith was the city's main quay for river traffic, a reminder that York was once a busy inland port. Today King's Staith, along with Lendal Bridge Landing, is the main embarkation point for the York Boat river trips.

LOWTHER

The King's Arms dates back to the seventeenth century, though it has been much rebuilt in both the nineteenth and twentieth centuries. It is probably one of York's most famous buildings, regularly featuring on the television news when the river is in flood.

King's Staith is generally the first area within the city to flood as the River Ouse levels rise. The prime riverside location makes it a popular spot on sunny summer days, provided the river hasn't breached the staith!

The river often reaches up to the windows of the King's Arms and a plaque just inside the door records the flood heights. The beer barrels are kept in the loft, rather than the cellar, to avoid flood damage. Originally a seventeenth-century customs house, it became the Kings Arm's in 1783, although it has gone through a number of name changes, reverting to the King's Arms in 1974. The pub sign depicts York's most famous Royal, Richard III.

Some fine eighteenth-century warehouses line the junction of King's Staith and Low Ousegate which drops down to Ouse Bridge.

Three Water Lanes ran from Castlegate, near St Mary's church, down to the Ouse at King's Staith. These lanes would have looked very much like the Shambles with overhanging – jettied – buildings. The lanes had some of the highest crime and poverty rates in the city and in 1852 the Corporation of York evicted the tenants and demolished the buildings.

The Guildhall was built between 1449 and 1453 for the Guild of St Christopher and the Corporation of York. It was very badly damaged during the Baedeker air-raids of the Second World War, but fully restored and reopened in 1960.

Lendal Tower was built soon after 1300 and formed part of the defensive walls around the city. Its principal role was to defend the weak spot around the river and to be the anchor for the huge iron chain that was hung across the Ouse to Barker Tower on the south bank and used to enforce river tolls during the Middle Ages.

In the seventeenth century, Lendal Tower became a waterworks, supplying fresh water to the city until 1846. The water tank was removed in the mid nineteenth century when the railway architect G.T. Andrews added the crenellated parapet.

In 1318 the Abbot of St Mary's Abbey sought consent to crenellate the abbey walls and to extend these down to the River Ouse. St Mary's River Tower was built around 1324, but though restored is left open to the elements.

Scarborough Railway Bridge was opened in 1845, but rebuilt in 1874. The recently restored LNER class A3 Pacific 60103 *Flying Scotsman* is seen crossing the River Ouse on a train bound for Scarborough.

British Railways Britannia class locomotive 70013 *Oliver Cromwell* is seen crossing the River Ouse on Scarborough Bridge on a Scarborough Spa Express service for Scarborough. Not the first time that Oliver Cromwell has entered the city!

LMS Jubilee class locomotive 5690 *Leander* heads for Scarborough on the Scarborough Spa Express.

CHAPTER 3
THE NORTH WEST QUARTER – AROUND THE MINSTER

The Yorkshire Museum was one of the first purpose-built museums in the country. Opening in 1830 and sponsored by the Yorkshire Philosophical Society, the museum and surrounding gardens were built in the grounds of St Mary's Abbey. Archaeology and science have been the principal themes for the museum since its inception and this remains true today. Most of the collection has been drawn from York and the surrounding North and East Ridings.

St Mary's Abbey was built by the Benedictine Order between 1270 and 1294 on the site of the previous Norman church. The abbey was being built at the same time as the current York Minster was under construction. The Benedictine monks were amongst the richest in the country at the time and the grandeur of the abbey reflected their wealth with towering arches and huge stained glass windows.

Inevitably, Henry VIII's Reformation would lead to the downfall of the abbey. The abbots were not particularly popular in York, living in luxury in the adjacent King's Manor, so there was little opposition when the abbots were accused of corruption by a Royal Commission. The abbey was dissolved in 1539.

As was the case across the country after the Reformation, the local population were quick to plunder the dissolved abbeys and the buildings quickly fell into a state of ruin. They were often used as a source of stone and other building materials for domestic properties in and around and St Mary's Abbey is no exception. Little remains today, but what does remain still presents a romantic ruin and complements the surrounding gardens.

All that remains of St Mary's Abbey today are the north and west walls. The ruins would have been much neglected throughout the rest of the sixteenth and seventeenth centuries, but by the eighteenth century there was a growing interest in these romantic ruins and contemporary painters and artists would often be drawn to paint and sketch what remained. In 1830 the abbey ruins were taken under the care of the Yorkshire Philosophical Society and today are maintained by the York Museums Trust.

The Hospitium is one of the few surviving abbey buildings, built as a place for visitors to the abbey to stay overnight, the name associated with hospitality. There is evidence that it might also have been used as a warehouse to store food. The ground floor is built of stone and would regularly have been subject to flooding, but now is protected by an earth bund. The Hospitium was restored in the late-nineteenth century by the Yorkshire Philosophical Society and is now a popular venue for functions, including weddings.

The Multangular Tower, a 10-sided Roman defensive structure, is thought to be York's oldest surviving building, potentially dating back to AD210. There was a legionary fortress on this site at the time and the tower was on the west corner of that fort. The lower courses of stone and brick are of Roman origin while the upper stone sections are medieval additions.

The Multangular Tower was designed to protrude from the fortress wall to enable defenders to target anyone attacking the adjacent walls. Such a construction would have made a real impression on the local tribes of the time, no doubt helping the Roman occupiers to subdue any potential unrest.

The Royal Family gifted the museum gardens to the Yorkshire Philosophical Society in 1828 and it was here that the society built the Yorkshire Museum to house the collection of archaeological finds. Creation of a botanical garden was a condition of the gift and the Society engaged the landscape architect Sir John Murray Naysmith to design the gardens. The gardens were opened to the public in 1835 and visited by the then Princess Victoria. In 1960 the gardens and the museum were given in trust to the City of York Council and are now managed by the York Museums Trust.

There are a number of archaeological treasures placed around the museum gardens including some Bronze Age rock art which came from the North York Moors. The rock art consists of cup and ring engravings, typical of the time and are likely to be about 4000 years old. There are a number of stone coffins scattered around the garden, including five Roman stone coffins within the Multangular Tower. They have all been sourced from graveyards across the city.

Admission to the museum gardens is free and during the spring and summer a variety of events and activities take place in the gardens, including open air theatre, festivals and Wild Wednesdays for children. The gardens are also home to the York Observatory which was built in 1832, the oldest working observatory in Yorkshire. Close to the entrance can be found the ruins of St Leonard's Hospital, the largest medieval hospital in Northern Britain, founded soon after the Norman Conquest. Along with the abbey, the hospital was destroyed in 1539 leaving York without a hospital for just over 200 years.

This former London Transport Routemaster double-decker bus now operates Ghostbustours around the centre of the city, complementing the half dozen ghost walks that tour the city on foot.

Right: King's Manor was built around 1270 to accommodate the abbots of the adjacent St Mary's Abbey, though much of the building that survives today is of fourteenth-century origin. After the Dissolution of the Monasteries following the Reformation, the building survived because Henry VIII decided that York would be the headquarters of the Council of the North. The buildings were therefore retained for this purpose.

King's Manor was the headquarters of the Council of the North until 1641 when the council was abolished. During the Civil War when York was under siege from the Parliamentarian army, as a Royalist garrison, the King's Manor was at the heart of some of the heavy fighting and casualties were accommodated within its walls. The coat of arms above the main doorway is that of Charles I.

After the Civil War the King's Manor became the residence for the Governor of York, but after 1688 the building was rented out to tenants and divided into separate accommodation.

From the nineteenth century the King's Manor became home to the Yorkshire School for the Blind until 1958 when the City of York Council bought the building and subsequently leased it to the University of York. Today the King's Manor is the home of the Department of Archaeology, the Centre for Medieval Studies and the Centre for Eighteenth Century Studies, a suitable home for students to absorb such subjects.

York City Art Gallery was built in 1879 to house the Yorkshire Fine Art Collection and today it is home to some of the paintings of York's most famous artist, William Etty, whose statue oversees the fountain in front of the main entrance. This is a fitting epitaph for Etty who campaigned to save many of York's historic buildings and we have him in part to thank for what survives today, including Bootham Bar, directly opposite where he now stands. The art gallery was closed for refurbishment in 2013 and reopened in 2015.

Bootham Bar dates originally to the eleventh century and the lower part of the structure is from this time. The upper tiers were added in the fourteenth century and the bar still has a portcullis which can be viewed when the walls are open. Unfortunately as with two of the other bars around York, the barbican was removed in 1832 as the Victorians sought to ease the pedestrian flow around the city. The bar suffered damage during the siege of York in 1644. The heads of traitors were sometimes displayed on the bar – the heads of three rebels who opposed the restoration of Charles II were displayed in this way in 1663.

Resembling its sister building at Fishergate, Bootham Postern, built in 1497, consists of a three-storey tower, a portion of wall some 3 feet thick, and a secondary gateway or postern. The tower and its postern marked the point at which the city walls met the precinct walls of the Abbey of St Mary. A 'postern' provided a secondary entrance to the city, through its walls.

St Mary's Tower was built in 1324 at the junction of Marygate and Bootham and forms part of the defensive walls around St Mary's Abbey. In 1318 the then abbot had sought permission to extend and crenellate the walls that surround the abbey. The tower was undermined during the Civil War when the Parliamentarian army laid siege to York and the huge crack is still clearly visible in the structure.

The Red House was built between 1702 and 1704 for Sir William Robinson, MP for York. The building is now an antiques centre. Local legend suggests that on his retirement from the role of Lord Mayor, Robinson refused to vacate the house and York Corporation was therefore forced into building the Mansion House in St Helen's Square.

Low Petergate offers fantastic views of the soaring west towers of York Minster and it is an archetypal medieval street, preserving some of that character of shopping streets of old with the retention of a number of individual shop signs. The 'Red Indian' is the traditional sign for a tobacconist's shop. Established in 1896, Barnitts *(top right)* is a York institution, essentially a hardware shop, but the kind of shop that is fast disappearing across the country. It retains a traditional approach and there's a strong chance that if you need something, Barnitts will have it.

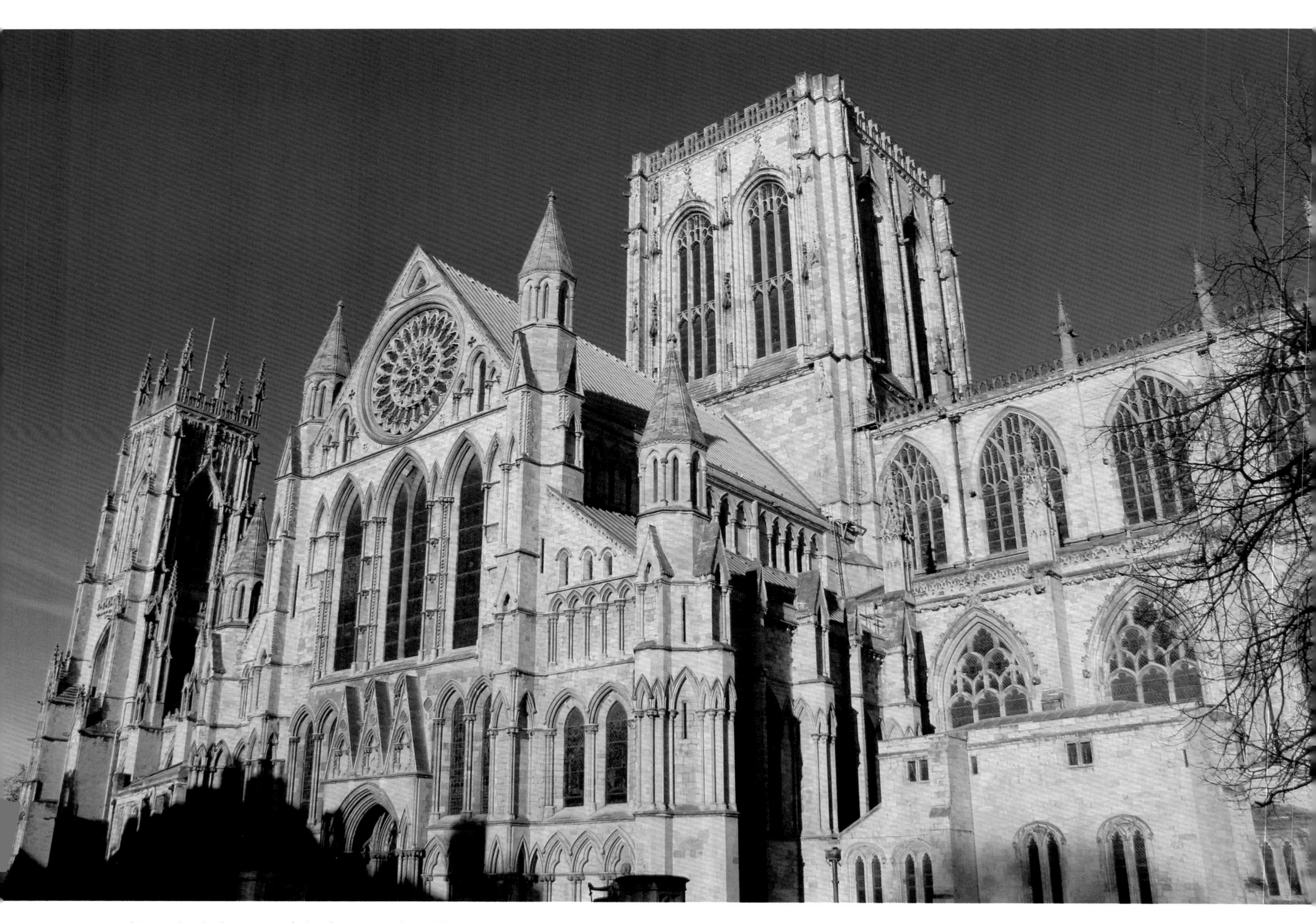

York's cathedral is one of the finest medieval buildings in Europe. York Minster is also known as St Peter's. It made national television news in 1984 when a huge fire took hold in the South Transept.

The Rose Window in the South Transept which overlooks Minster Gates is one of the most famous stained glass windows in Britain. It was badly damaged in the 1984 fire. Much of the stained glass survived and there are still pieces that date to the sixteenth and eighteenth centuries.

There has been a church on this site since AD627 and the stone Saxon church survived until the Norman occupation when it was destroyed by William the Conqueror's invading army. It took over 250 years to build the current Minster, with work starting in 1220 and not complete until 1472. This is the spectacular West Front seen from Duncombe Place.

The Great West Window was built in 1330 and dominates the western end of the nave when seen from within the Minster. The Great West Front stands tall over Duncombe Place.

York's only surviving gas lamps still light the entrance below the West Front.

The Minster employs its own stonemasons and their masonry yard is directly below the Minster in Dean's Place, where members of the public can watch these skilled craftsmen at work. Erosion of the soft magnesian limestone takes its toll on the outer face of the Minster and over the centuries countless stone setts and statues have been replaced.

Visitors are welcome to climb to the top of the central tower, although as part of an organised tour. There are several scheduled ascents each day and on a sunny day the view across York is unrivalled. On a clear day, the views extend to the Pennines, the North York Moors and the Yorkshire Wolds.

One of few statues in York, this one of Roman Emperor Constantine has graced the South Transept of York Minster since 1998. Constantine became Emperor in AD306 during his visit to York. He converted to Christianity six years later.

Right: Although since dismantled, the Wheel of York offered excellent views of York Minster and its dominant position from a different perspective.

The view from the central tower extends to the Yorkshire Wolds. York has typically had strong allegiances with the East Riding of Yorkshire.

The Deanery was built as recently as 1940 for the Dean of York.

This statue of St Peter to whom the Minster is dedicated illustrates the extensive corrosion that magnesian limestone can suffer. Quarried locally near Tadcaster, a new statue was carved to replace this original from about 1400.

Below: Today known as the Old Palace or Minster Library, this building was the old chapel of the Archbishop of York and was built in the thirteenth century. It is a Grade II listed building.

Dean's Park was originally reserved solely for the clergy, but today is open to the public during daylight hours. The Minster Close still operates its own police force to patrol the Minster environs, completely independent of the North Yorkshire Police. Dean's Park is also home to the war memorial which occupies the twelfth-century arcade seen here.

The archway leads to the former Purey-Cust Hospital, like so many such buildings, now a private residence. The hospital opened in 1915. The coat of arms with the black raven is that of the former Dean of York, Arthur Purey-Cust who was Dean from 1880 to 1916.

Dean's Park is an oasis of calm within the city. It is popular with office workers and visitors seeking some quiet from the hustle and bustle of the main streets.

Treasurer's House has been in the care of the National Trust since 1930. The house takes its name from the medieval house of the Minster Treasurer which was close by. The house we see today was largely built in the early seventeenth century, including the symmetrical front that overlooks the walled garden. There are medieval foundations in the basement which date back to the fourteenth century.

Treasurer's House was built on an old Roman Road and in 1953, a local plumber, Harry Martindale, while working in the basement, claimed to have witnessed a small troop of Roman soldiers with horse and cart emerge from a supporting wall and march through the cellar, initially visible only from the knees up.

St William's College was founded in 1455 to provide accommodation for the chantry priests of York Minster. The half-timbered, jettied building was built in 1465 and the impressive front hides an attractive courtyard behind the main entrance door.

The building was confiscated during the Dissolution of the Monasteries and was used largely as a private residence until restoration in the early twentieth century and it subsequently returned to the care of the Dean and Chapter of York Minster in 1972. The building is named after William Fitzherbert who was Archbishop of York from 1143 to 1172.

Left: The Snickleway Inn is a fifteenth-century galleried inn and one of the oldest and most historic pubs in York. The Snickleway is the most recent name that this public house has carried, named after Mark W. Jones' book on the snickelways of York. The inn has previously been known as the House of Tudor. During the Civil War and the siege of York the pub was used as a magazine for Royalist troops. It is supposedly the most haunted pub in York.

Right: The Golden Slipper public house is a much altered medieval building dating originally from the fifteenth century. The Victorian brick façade was added in the nineteenth century. During restoration work in 1984, a medieval slipper was found by workmen and put on display.

Lady Row dates from 1316 and is the earliest row of houses surviving in the city. The row hides Holy Trinity church almost completely from view. The houses were built in what was the original churchyard, built for chantry priests and the jettied overhang feature is thought to be the oldest example of its kind in England.

The timbered projection that extends from the National Trust shop is thought to be the remains of a covered bridge built across Goodramgate in 1396 to enable the vicars choral to access the Minster from Bedern without having to run the gauntlet of the medieval streets.

Holy Trinity is one of York's most delightful secrets. Hidden away behind Lady Row in a walled, leafy churchyard, this is one of the city's best preserved churches. Founded in the late eleventh century, the present church dates mainly from the fifteenth century. Step inside and you are immediately transported back to Georgian times. Holy Trinity is the only church in the city to have retained its box pews. The church is no longer in use as a place of worship and today is in the care of the Churches Conservation Trust.

As with Bootham Bar, Monk Bar retains its portcullis, the only one that can still be lowered if required. The portcullis was last lowered in 1953 to celebrate the coronation of Queen Elizabeth II. The bar, which dates from the early fourteenth century, now houses the Richard III Museum. Monk Bar is the largest and most ornate of the bars.

The wall in the section between Monk Gate and Jewbury is thought to follow the line of Viking and Norman ramparts as the Roman occupiers built their defences much straighter.

Ice houses were popular in the late eighteenth century and this one is thought to have been built around 1800. They were packed with ice in the cold winter months and insulated so that ice would be available all through the year.

The New Tower, built in 1380, marks the point where the wall makes a dramatic turn to protect the church of St Cuthbert which sits directly behind the tower at this point.

There are many places in Yorkshire that lay claim to the Robin Hood legend – from Robin Hood's Bay on the Yorkshire Coast to Robin Hood's Bed up on the Pennine Moors. Robin Hood's Tower just behind the Minster is a Victorian re-construction and the link to one of England's most famous outlaws is not clear.

Merchant Taylors Hall is the only surviving craft guild hall in York. The main fabric of the building dates back to around 1400, though it was much refurbished in the late seventeenth and early eighteenth centuries. The Company of Merchant Taylors is one of three guilds in York that can trace an unbroken history back to medieval times.

Aldwark is a gently curving street that connects Peasholme Green to Colliergate. There are a number of interesting buildings located on Aldwark, including Oliver Sheldon House, an attractive early-eighteenth century Georgian double-fronted house and York's first purpose built Methodist chapel. Built in 1759, the chapel had a short life and closed in 1804.

St Anthony's Hall in York is a former medieval guildhall and Grade I listed building. The hall was built between 1446 and 1453 on the site of a chapel of St Anthony for either the Guild of St Martin or the Guild of St Anthony. Between 1627 and 1705 it saw use as an arsenal, a military hospital and a prison. Between 1705 and 1947 it housed the York Bluecoat School, after which it was offered to the York Civic Trust. In 1953, it became the Borthwick Institute for Historical Research, but since 2008 it has been home to the Quilt Museum and Gallery.

St Cuthbert's church was mentioned in the Domesday Book and some of the original eleventh-century sections incorporate Roman masonry. Much of the rest of the church dates to the fifteenth century.

Right: Lady Hewley's Almshouses were built on St Saviourgate in 1840 in a Tudor style.

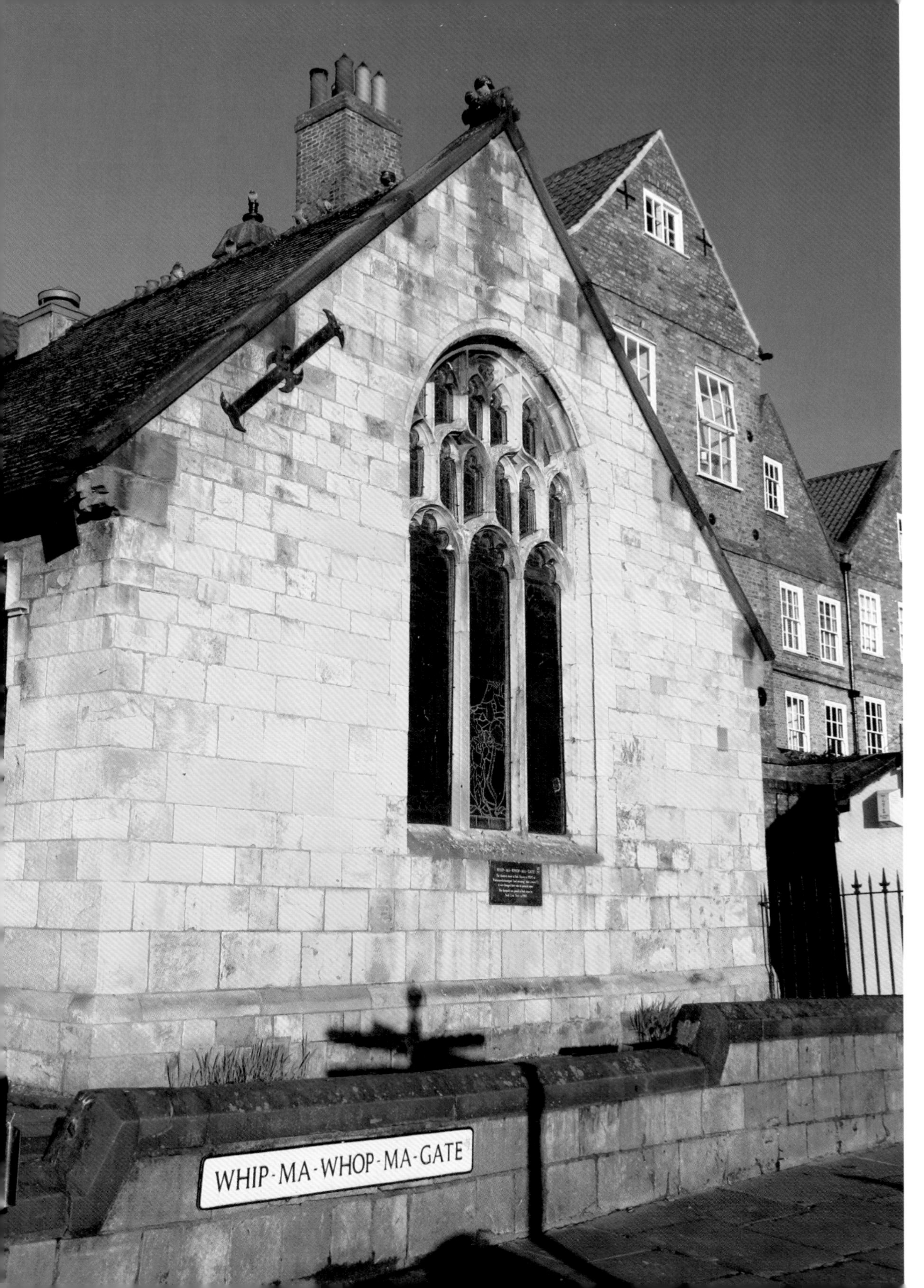

Whip-Ma-Whop-Ma-Gate is one of the smallest streets in York. The origin of the unusual name is not clear. As with many of York's inner streets, 'Gate' has its origins in the Norse word 'gata' which means street. One suggestion is that it is a corruption of 'Whitnourwhatnourgate' which simply means 'What a street!'. There has also been a whipping post and stocks on the site which may have also influenced the name.

St Crux church was also mentioned in the Domesday Book. It was demolished in 1887 and this parish room was built on the site the following year incorporating part of the north wall of the original church.

The Centenary Methodist Church was opened in 1840, a remarkably showy piece of architecture for the Wesleyan faith. It is in a Greek style with striking Ionic columns flanking the main entrance.

The Shambles is one of York's older streets and possibly its most famous. It has a good number of overhanging timber-framed buildings, some dating back as far as the fourteenth century. It perhaps epitomises our modern view of what a typical medieval street looked like.

The street was once known as The Great Flesh Shambles, probably from the Anglo-Saxon Flesh-ammels, after the shelves that butchers used to display their meat. As recently as 1872 25 butchers' shops were located along the street; today there are none. Some of the meat hooks used to suspend cuts of meat can still be seen on some of the shop fronts.

No.10 and 11 on the Shambles is a shrine to Saint Margaret Clitherow, who was married to a butcher who owned and lived in a shop there. A practising Catholic, she met her death after the discovery of a priest hole by the fireplace.

Right: The rooftop view of High Petergate, Stonegate and Low Petergate illustrates how tightly packed the medieval core of York is.

Jubbergate is a small street close to Newgate Market. The timbered building is a mix of fourteenth- and seventeenth-century origin and it was heavily restored in the early 1930s. During the recent refurbishment of Newgate Market, new views were opened up of the rear of the timber-framed houses that line the Shambles. There have been markets in York since the eighth century. The current Newgate Market dates to 1964 when it relocated from Parliament Street.

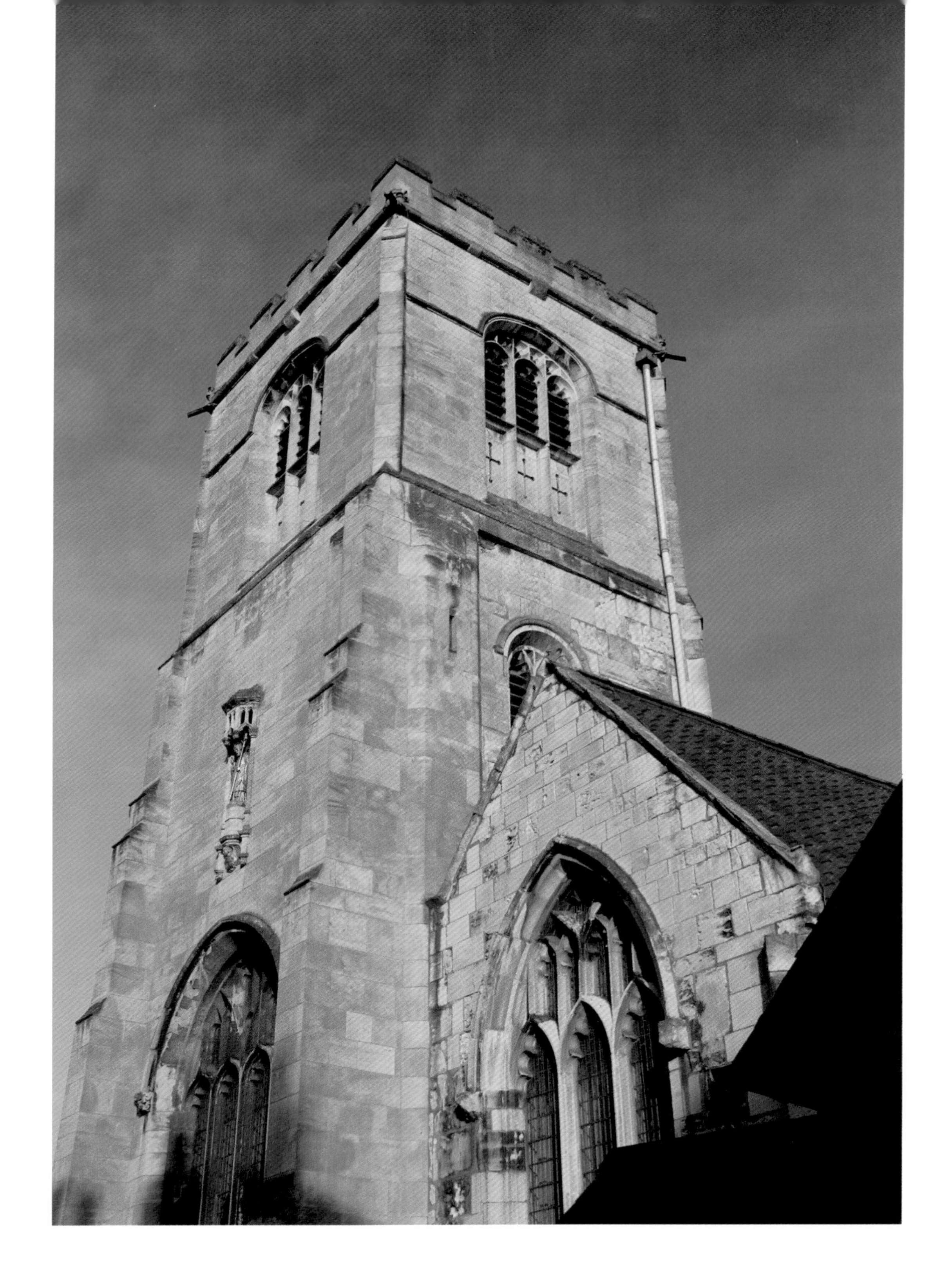

St Sampson's church has its origins in 1154, but the current building dates largely to the 1440s. It is no longer in use as a place of worship, but like many of York's churches, the building has found another use. Today it is home to St Sampson's Centre for the Over '60s.

This Roman Column was recovered from the undercroft beneath York Minster when the foundations for the Minster were being underpinned and strengthened. The column is located in Minster Yard close to the Minster School and St Michael-le-Belfrey. The current church dates from 1537.

Stonegate is on the line of the old Roman Via Praetoria and the origin of the name is either because it was one of the first stone paved streets in York or because it was the route along which the magnesian limestone quarried in Tadcaster was brought to build the Minster. It is reputedly the birthplace of Guy Fawkes, though at least two buildings lay claim to this. Stonegate hides a number of interesting features, including the remains of York's oldest house, a Norman stone house behind No.50, an old ship's figurehead in recognition of York's past importance as a port, York's oldest pub – Ye Olde Starre Inn, a Dutch Coat of Arms and some eighteenth-century firemarks which indicated to the private fire service whether you had paid your insurance or not and therefore whether they would or would not save your building if it was on fire!

The Red Devil is the traditional sign for a printer's shop. Stonegate was once the centre of York's printing industry. York's first printer came here in 1480.

Mulberry Hall was built in 1434, a timber-framed building which has been a shop since at least the eighteenth century.

Stonegate is generally one of the busier shopping streets in York and is a good example of how the city has preserved its historic character while balancing the needs of today's consumer society.

Barley Hall was reconstructed by the York Archaeological Trust in the early 1990s on the site of a fourteenth-century hospice. Not much of the original fourteenth and fifteenth century building remains, though some elements were incorporated into the newly constructed hall. Coffee Yard is another excellent example of the intriguing snickelways that can be found around York linking various streets.

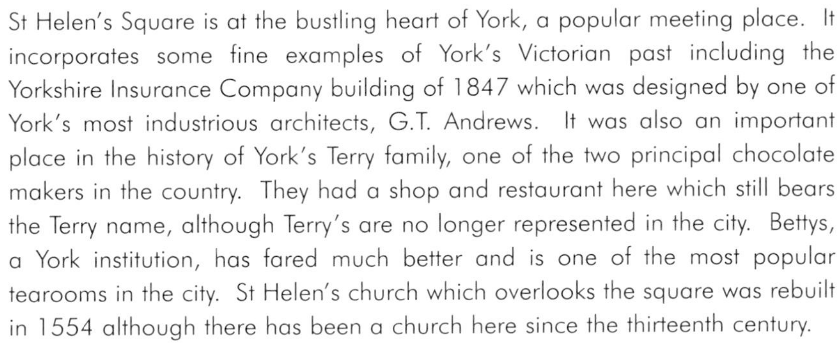

St Helen's Square is at the bustling heart of York, a popular meeting place. It incorporates some fine examples of York's Victorian past including the Yorkshire Insurance Company building of 1847 which was designed by one of York's most industrious architects, G.T. Andrews. It was also an important place in the history of York's Terry family, one of the two principal chocolate makers in the country. They had a shop and restaurant here which still bears the Terry name, although Terry's are no longer represented in the city. Bettys, a York institution, has fared much better and is one of the most popular tearooms in the city. St Helen's church which overlooks the square was rebuilt in 1554 although there has been a church here since the thirteenth century.

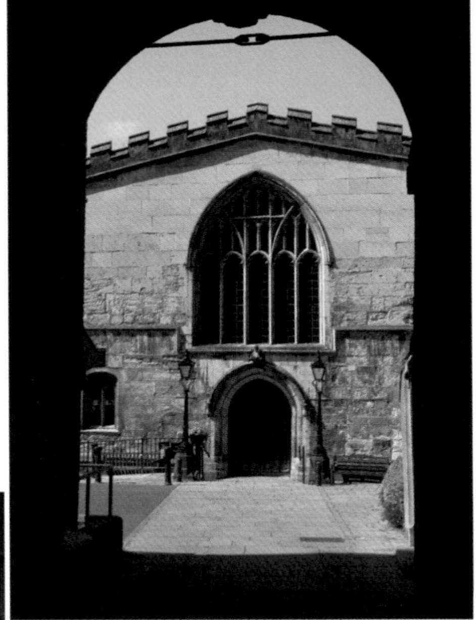

The Guildhall was built in 1445 for the 'Guild of St Christopher and St George' and the Corporation. Council meetings are still held here. The hall was badly damaged by German bombs during the so-called Baedeker Raid of 1942. It took eighteen years before the stone shell of the Guildhall was restored. It was re-opened by Queen Elizabeth, the Queen Mother on 21 June 1960.

The Mansion House was built between 1725 and 1730 and remarkably for such a grand public building, the records of the architect who designed the building are lost. It is probably the work of William Etty. It was England's first purpose-built mayoral residence and it still performs a civic function today.

One of the main shopping streets in York, there will be few shoppers and visitors who look up and notice the figure known as the 'Little Admiral' who stands on top of the clock outside St Martin-le-Grand church on Coney Street. He's holding a cross staff; an early form of sextant. The church and clock were badly damaged by the 1942 German air raid along with the adjacent Guildhall.

CHAPTER 4

THE NORTH EAST QUARTER – AROUND THE CASTLE

All Saints church in Pavement was mentioned in the Domesday Book, but the current church largely dates from the late fourteenth century. The lantern tower dates from around 1400. The tower was lit to guide travellers to York through the Forest of Galtres which surrounded the northern approaches to York in earlier times. 34 Lord Mayors of York have been buried here.

The Golden Fleece pub is one of York's oldest inns. There has been a pub on this site since at least 1503 and the building is thought to be sixteenth century. It is possible that the Golden Fleece was named in honour of the some of the guildsmen of the nearby Merchant Adventurers Hall who traded in fleece and wool. It is reputedly one of York's most haunted inns.

Pavement was one of the earliest paved streets in York. The half-timbered and jettied Herbert House is thought to have been built in 1620 by John Jacques, a local merchant. It was fully restored in 1926, an early example of restoration of one of York's historic buildings.

Lady Peckett's Yard is one of York's most appealing 'snickelways' and leads from Pavement through to Fossgate. The jettied medieval building that overhangs the yard is mid sixteenth century. It is named in honour of Alice Peckett, wife of John Peckett, who was Lord Mayor of York in 1701.

The Black Swan was built for William Bowes, a merchant and Sheriff of York in 1417. Bowes later became Lord Mayor in 1428. By the late sixteenth century the building was in use as a public house and was greatly extended in the seventeenth century. It is reputed to have a number of ghosts. Peasholme Green used to be a water meadow where peas were grown, a common agricultural crop around York today.

Rowntree Wharf was built by Henry Leetham in 1860 and at the time was one of the largest flour mills in Europe. With a castellated tower, it was built between the River Foss and Wormald's Cut, a short purpose built canal, and grain was brought in by barge. The mill closed in 1930 and the building was later used by Rowntree and Company as their Navigation Warehouse. It closed in the 1960s and in the late 1980s was converted into apartments by the Joseph Rowntree Foundation. The tall chimney is all that remains of York's power station and refuse destructor which was located on Foss Islands Road. It dates from 1899 and is now a Grade II listed structure.

There are few derelict warehouses around York that haven't been converted into apartments or offices. This example on Navigation Road was served by Wormald's Cut, a short canal that branches off the River Foss. The Foss Navigation Company canalised the River Foss from 1778 and it was eventually made navigable as far as Sheriff Hutton. River trade has always been important for York and archaeological excavations have revealed evidence of jetties and wharves that date back to Roman times.

Dorothy Wilson's Hospital on Walmgate was originally built as an almshouse in the early eighteenth century. Wilson died in 1719 and left funds in her will for the provision of an almshouse and school. It was rebuilt in 1765 and then again in 1812.
Inset: York has always had strong links with the East Riding and today those links are maintained and York is still an important centre for work, shopping and leisure for people who live in East Yorkshire. East Yorkshire Motor Services still connect remote Yorkshire Wolds villages with York.

There is more to York history than Romans, Vikings and Medieval monarchs. Our more recent history can sometimes still be found, but regrettably is disappearing fast. After 93 years of trading, the Army and Navy Stores in Fossgate closed in 2012. The shop has since been sympathetically refurbished as a bar incorporating some of the shop's original features, but another link with the past has been lost.

The Blue Bell is one of York's smallest pubs and still retains many of its original features. The building dates from 1798 and the tiled front hides a cosy, Edwardian interior. There are two small rooms inside, both wood panelled and a discrete serving hatch at the bar for customers in the back room.

The Electric Theatre was York's first purpose-built cinema. Built in 1911 it is now a furniture store.

Merchant Adventurers Hall is one of the best preserved guild houses in the country. Originally built for the Guild of Our Lord Jesus and the Blessed Virgin Mary, much of the hall dates from the mid fourteenth century. This guild was later incorporated into the Guild of Mercers and Merchants which by the late sixteenth century had become the Company of Merchant Adventurers of the City of York.

The Merchant Adventurers Hall on Fossgate was built between 1357 and 1368 on the site of a Norman mansion as a communal meeting hall, chapel and undercroft hospital. The hall is framed in oak from the Forest of Galtres.

The Great Hall and undercroft largely date from the mid fourteenth century. Over time the floor of the undercroft has been raised to protect the building from the inevitable flooding from the adjacent River Foss. The gatehouse to Merchant Adventurers Hall was built in the mid seventeenth century though the elaborate coat of arms above the door was renewed in the mid nineteenth century.

The Red Tower dates from 1490 and marked the end of the city walls, as beyond that point the King's Fishpool acted as a deterrent to any potential attacking army. The building has subsided over the years such that the masonry foundations are no longer visible. The building was controversial at the time in being constructed of brick rather than masonry, which led to violence between the two groups of craftsmen. The building has been used subsequently as a gunpowder store and is occasionally opened to the public on heritage weekends.

Walmgate Bar is the only one of York's four bars to retain its outer barbican. Built in the twelfth century, the barbican was added 200 years later. A small wooden dwelling was added in the Elizabethan era and remained occupied until 1957. A coffee house now occupies the upper two storeys of the bar, giving visitors an opportunity to study and enjoy this fine surviving medieval defensive structure for the price of a cuppa. Walmgate Bar was heavily damaged during the Civil War and restored in 1646.

Fishergate Bar is one of the additional breaches made in the city walls in 1315 to ease the flow of pedestrians into and out of the city and to control trade. It was blocked up in 1489 after fire damage was sustained during rioting and some of the reddened stonework from that fire can still be seen today. It was unblocked and refurbished in the early eighteenth century when much of the city walls were improved.

The eighteenth-century Highwayman Dick Turpin was executed at York's Tyburn on the Knavesmire on 7 April 1739. His real name was John Palmer and he was far from the romantic image of a highwayman that has developed in later times. He was arrested at the George and Dragon pub in Welton near Hull and brought to York for trial and hanged on the gallows.

Fishergate Postern isn't regularly open to the public, but access is occasionally granted to this three-storey tower during heritage open weekends. The tower was built between 1504 and 1507, although it incorporates a fourteenth-century archway.

St Denys church was founded in the mid to late twelfth century and retains an attractive Norman arched doorway. As with much of the Walmgate area, it was heavily damaged by Parliamentarian troops during the siege of York. York was a Royalist headquarters during the Civil War.

Raindale Mill is a reconstructed early-nineteenth-century flour mill which was moved from the North York Moors to the grounds of York Castle Museum in the 1960s.

William the Conqueror built two motte and bailey castles in York between 1068 and 1069, an indication of the high strategic value of the city. The castle was rebuilt in stone between 1245 and 1315. The remains of the late-thirteenth-century bailey wall together with the two round south and southeast towers still survive next to the River Foss. The castle became redundant after the English Civil War and was largely demolished.

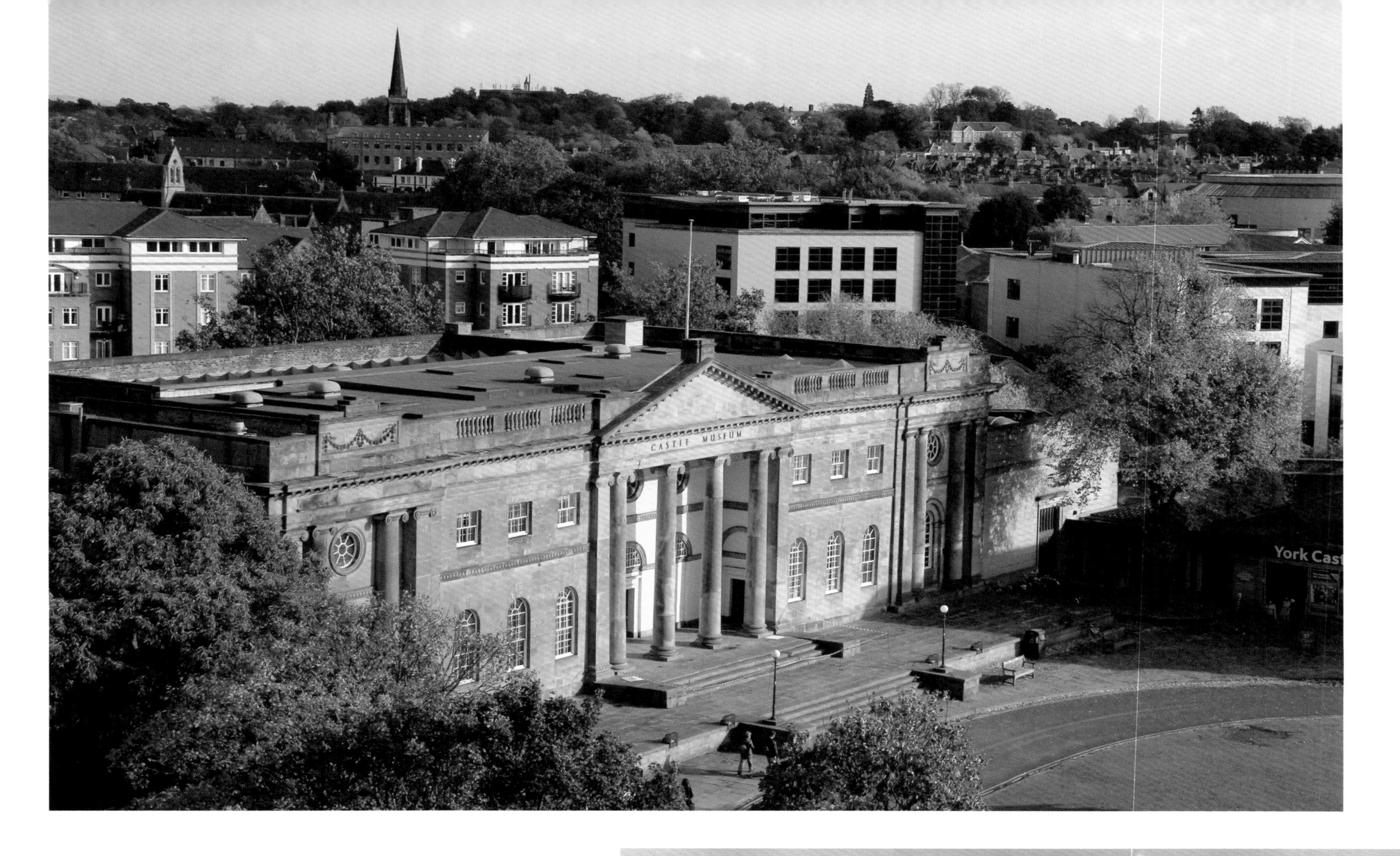

Following the demolition of York Castle, the bailey was used as the site for two new prisons and the Assize Courts. The debtor's prison was opened in 1705 and the female prison later in 1780. The Assize Court building was opened in 1777. York Castle Museum was founded in 1938 by Dr John Kirk, an amateur archaeologist who was a member of the Yorkshire Archaeology Society. The Castle Museum incorporates both the female prison and debtor's prison, which by 1938 had closed. The Assize Court remains in use today.

Clifford's Tower is unique in the British Isles, a quatrefoil design that had first seen use in France in the mid twelfth century. It was built in the thirteenth century on one of the two mottes constructed by William the Conqueror between 1068 and 1069. Clifford's Tower is thought to take its name from Henry Clifford. Clifford was Constable of York Castle in the seventeenth century and the forebuilding bears his coat of arms carved in stone.

The entrance forebuilding at Clifford's Tower largely dates from around 1642. From that date it was used as a garrison until 1684 when it was gutted by fire. The reddening of the stone from the fire can still be seen today. By the eighteenth century the ruined tower had become derelict and covered in vegetation, by then a romantic ruin within the grounds of a private residence. Today it is in the care of English Heritage.

On the night of Friday 16 March 1190, some 150 Jews from York sought refuge in the wooden castle that stood on this site at that time. They were looking for protection from a mob who had been whipped up into an anti-Semitic demonstration. They chose to die at their own hands rather than renounce their faith. The daffodils are regularly in flower at the anniversary of the atrocity.

This 25 pounder field gun stands sentinel over Clifford's Tower on the steps of the Castle Museum.

Clifford's Tower has regularly been a venue for the York Illuminated Festival held annually at the end of October and beginning of November. Images are projected onto the tower walls to tell York's story.

There was a moat surrounding York Castle and during the devastating floods of 2012 and 2015 the River Ouse burst its banks and almost reached the base of Clifford's Tower, recreating the impression of a moat.

Fairfax House is thought to date back to the early 1740s. After years of use as a cinema and dancehall, the building was restored by York Civic Trust in the early 1980s and now houses a fine display of Georgian furniture, part of Noel Terry's Collection.

Fairfax House was bought by the Viscount Fairfax of Emely in 1759 and transformed by the notable York Architect John Carr into a fashionable townhouse for the Fairfax family who were normally resident at Gilling Castle, 20 miles north of York.

CHAPTER 5
OUTWITH THE WALLS

The current York railway station was the third station to be built in York and opened in 1877 as rail traffic on the East Coast Main Line increased, necessitating a move outside the city walls. The grand overall station roof was designed by North Eastern Railway architects Thomas Prosser and William Peachey. At the time of its opening, York Station was the largest railway station in Europe. LNER A4 class locomotive 60009 *Union Of South Africa* arrives with a special for Scarborough.

British Railways A1 class locomotive 60163 *Tornado* awaits departure from York Station with a Cathedrals Express return service to London Kings Cross.

This Deltic diesel locomotive replaced the famous A4 class steam locomotives on fast express trains on the East Coast Main Line. Here Deltic D9000 *Royal Scots Grey* arrives at York with an Edinburgh to Kings Cross special excursion. These diesel locomotives were retired from regular service in 1982.

Left: British Railways Britannia class locomotive 70013 *Oliver Cromwell* is seen awaiting departure from York Station with a Scarborough Spa Express service for Scarborough.

The National Railway Museum was opened in 1975 on the site of the old Motive Power Depot which once housed the great express passenger locomotives that operated up and down the East Coast Main Line. The museum houses the National Collection from railway locomotives, carriages and wagons to railwayana, as well as an extensive document archive. One of the recent highlights was in 2013 when all surviving A4 class express locomotives were gathered from around the UK and Canada and the USA for display. The railway museum is normally only home to the famous A4 *Mallard* which achieved the world steam speed record in 1938 when it reached 126mph, a record it still holds to this day.

The National Railway Museum regularly takes part in the York Illuminated autumn festival. In Autumn 2013 the highlight was the Great Gathering of A4 class express locomotives to mark the 75th anniversary of *Mallard* achieving the world steam speed record. The streamlined LNER A4 Pacifics were put on display alongside the LMS Coronation class streamlined Pacific *Duchess of Hamilton* in a celebration of speed and style.

Holgate tower windmill was built in 1770. After storm damage in 1930, the mill stopped grinding under wind power and the sails and the fantail were removed. Milling production stopped completely in 1933. Although the mill was given Grade II listed building status in 1954, it remained disused. In 2001 the Holgate Preservation Society was formed, and the mill was opened to the public in 2005. Restoration began in 2003 and was completed in April 2012 when the sails turned, powered by wind, for the first time since 1930.

Rowntree Park is a 20-acre park created as a memorial to the employees of Rowntree's who lost their lives during the First World War. It was opened in 1921 by local entrepreneur and philanthropist Joseph Rowntree. The gates at the riverbank entrance are eighteenth century and were given by the company as a memorial to the people of York who died in the Second World War.

Ingram Hospital in Bootham was built between 1630 and 1632 and consists of eleven bays of two storeys and a tall four-storey tower. The tower incorporates a Norman doorway which is thought to have come from Holy Trinity Priory in Micklegate. It was built as almshouses and damaged during the Civil War siege of York. In more recent times the building has been refurbished by the York Conservation Trust.

St Peter's School was founded AD627 and is the third oldest school in the UK. The school was originally located within the precincts of York Minster, but moved to the current site in 1838 when it merged with York Proprietary School from nearby Clifton. Today the school is a co-educational independent boarding and day school. Guy Fawkes is one of St Peter's most famous alumni; he studied at the school in 1575.

York St John University became a fully fledged university able to award degrees in 2006, although the university has its origins in two former Anglican teacher training colleges established in 1841 for men and five years later for women. Over time the education programme was extended to cover wider topics and the college developed into the College of Ripon and York St John. The buildings date back to 1845-6 and were designed by G.T. Andrews who went on to work for the York and North Midland Railway.

End of terrace painted adverts were once common across industrialised Northern Britain. Largely redundant and replaced by poster billboards, a number of painted adverts can still be found across York, this notable example being on Lord Mayor's Walk.

The medieval tower of St Lawrence church survives in the grounds of its Victorian replacement on Hull Road. The original church was built in the twelfth century, though the tower was extended in both the thirteenth and fifteenth centuries. The replacement church was built in 1881-3.

Heslington Hall is a Grade II listed rebuilt manor house near the village of Heslington. The hall is now part of the campus of the University of York. The original manor house was built in 1568 for Sir Thomas Eynns. The hall was rebuilt in 1854 by the architect Philip Hardwick. At the outbreak of the Second World War, the house was vacated by the family and it was taken over by the Royal Air Force as the headquarters of No. 4 Group RAF, part of RAF Bomber Command. After the war the family did not return to the hall and when the University of York opened in 1963, Heslington Hall became the administrative headquarters of the University.

The Knavesmire is in part occupied by York Racecourse and races have been held here since 1731. The wider Knavesmire is one of a number of undeveloped, uncultivated strays around York, which offers green open spaces with access for all. The Knavesmire was also home to York's version of Tyburn and the gallows was located close to where Tadcaster Road is today. Dick Turpin was hanged here in 1739 with the last public hanging held in 1801.

Imphal Barracks on Fulford Road were built between 1877 and 1880 although there have been cavalry barracks on this site since 1795. The barracks are named after the Battle of Imphal in 1944 and are the current home of the 4th Infantry Brigade.

The Chocolate Works factory opened in 1926, where over the years it manufactured Terry's Chocolate Orange, Terry's All Gold and York Fruits. Terry's was acquired by Kraft Foods in 1993, who decided to switch production of remaining products to factories in Europe. The factory closed in September 2005. Today the site is being redeveloped as luxury apartments.

Bishopthorpe Palace has been the home of the Archbishops of York for over 750 years. The village was originally known as St Andrewthorpe, but became Bishopthorpe in the thirteenth century when the archbishop purchased the local manor house. The current Bishopthorpe Palace was built on the site between 1763 and 1769 and is a Grade I listed building.